Light makes life possible.

Without light:

- the world would be dark.
- we could not see.
- plants could not grow.
- everything would be cold.

But what is light?
Where does it come from?

Light is a form of energy we can see.
It travels through space.

Most of our light comes from the sun.
The sun is our closest star.
It is 92 million miles away.

The light travels through space to earth.
It travels in a straight line.
See the path of light for yourself.

All About Light

by Melvin Berger
illustrated by Blanche Sims

SCHOLASTIC INC.
New York   Toronto   London   Auckland   Sydney

For Max
— M.B.

To Mark Hoyt, with love
— B.S.

ISBN 0-590-48076-6

Text copyright © 1995 by Melvin Berger
Illustrations copyright © 1995 by Scholastic Inc.
All rights reserved. Published by Scholastic Inc.

12 11 10 9 8 7 6 5 4 3 2   6 7 8 9/9 0/0

Printed in the U.S.A.   23

First Scholastic printing, June 1995

DO IT YOURSELF

See the Light

Get a straight drinking straw.
Turn on a lamp.
Look at the bulb through the straw.
Can you see the light?

Now bend the straw.
Look again.
What happens?
You cannot see the light.
That's because light cannot turn.
It cannot go through a bent straw.

Light can't turn a corner.
But it can bounce.
Try it out.

DO IT YOURSELF

Bouncing Balls, Bouncing Light

Drop a round ball straight down.
What happens to the ball?
It bounces straight up.

Shine a flashlight straight at a mirror.
What do you see?
The light bounces off the mirror.
The light comes straight back at you.

Now throw the ball at a slant.
What happens?
The ball bounces back at a slant.

Shine the flashlight at the mirror again.
But shine it at a slant.
The light bounces back at you on a slant.

Light that bounces back is called reflected light.
You are reading this book by reflected light.
The light comes from the sun or a lightbulb.
The light hits the book.
Some of the light is reflected back.

The reflected light enters your eyes.
Your eyes send out electrical signals
that travel to your brain.
Your brain changes the signals into words.

But light is not always reflected.
Some objects let light pass right through.
These objects are called transparent.
Glass is transparent.
Water and air are transparent, too.

Some objects let only a little light pass through.
These objects are called translucent.
Wax paper is translucent.
Frosted glass and clouds are translucent, too.

Some objects let no light pass through.
These objects are called opaque.
A piece of wood is opaque.
Metal and cardboard are opaque, too.

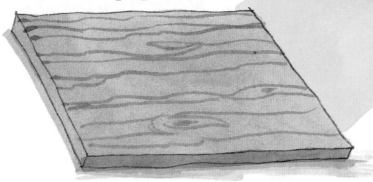

DO IT YOURSELF

Transparent, Translucent, Opaque

Get a flashlight.
Walk around your house in the evening.
Shine your flashlight through different things.

Shine your flashlight through:

- a paper towel.
- a glass of water.
- a piece of plastic wrap.
- a piece of aluminum foil.
- a dish.
- a piece of tissue paper.

Transparent

Translucent

Opaque

Which objects let the light through?
They are transparent.
The glass of water and plastic wrap are transparent.

Which objects let only some light through?
They are translucent.
The paper towel and tissue paper are translucent.

Which objects let no light through?
They are opaque.
The aluminum foil and the dish are opaque.

Water is transparent.
But water can change light in strange ways.

DO IT YOURSELF

See Light Bend

Take a pencil.
Place it in a half glass of water.
Look at the pencil from the side.
Does it look as if the pencil is broken?

Take the pencil out.
The pencil is not broken.
It only looked broken.
The water bent the reflected light
from the pencil.

Did you know that your eye also bends light?
The front part of your eye is called the lens.
You have a lens in each eye.
Lenses are transparent.
They are also curved.
Lenses bend light.
They help you see clearly.

You can see clearly close-up.
And you can see clearly far away.
How do your lenses make this possible?

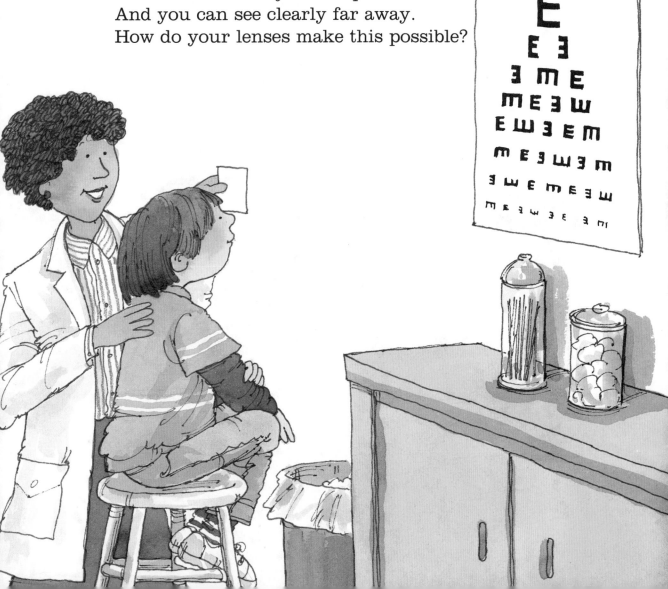

DO IT YOURSELF

How Lenses Work

Stare at this book.
Then suddenly look out the window.
Do you feel something change inside your eye?

Tiny muscles pull on the lenses.
The muscles change the shape of the lenses.

When you look at the book, your lenses
are thick.
When you look at something far away,
your lenses become thinner.

Lenses are in your eyes.
But you can also find lenses in:

- magnifying glasses and eyeglasses.
- microscopes and telescopes.
- cameras and projectors.

These lenses are made of glass or clear plastic.
They make objects look larger or smaller.
They also make objects look clearer or fuzzier.

MAGNIFYING GLASS

EYEGLASSES

MICROSCOPE

TELESCOPE

CAMERA

PROJECTOR

DO IT YOURSELF

Lenses of Glass and Plastic

Look at a word on this page.
Use your eyes alone.
Then look at it through a magnifying glass.
Next, look at it through an eyeglass lens.

Both kinds of lenses bend the light.
They change the way the words look.

Your eyes also let you see different colors.
But do you know where colors come from?

Most of the light around you is white light.
White light is made up of different colors.
It is made up of primary colors — red, yellow,
and blue.
And of secondary colors — orange, green,
and violet.

Have you ever seen a rainbow in the sky?
The best time is when the sun shines after
a rain shower.
Sometimes drops of water are still in the air.
The water drops bend the sun's white light.
They break the light into different colors.
A rainbow appears.

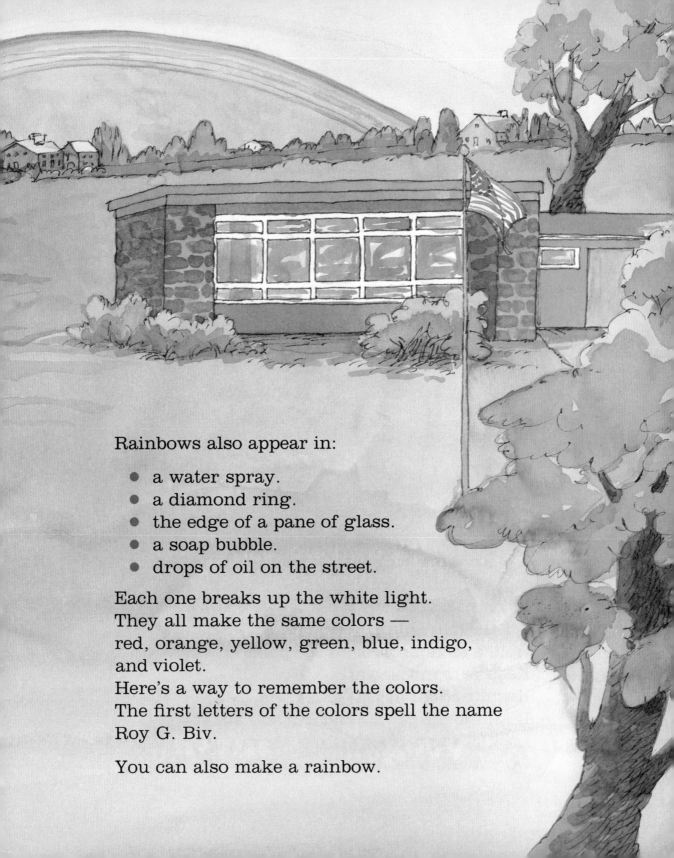

Rainbows also appear in:

- a water spray.
- a diamond ring.
- the edge of a pane of glass.
- a soap bubble.
- drops of oil on the street.

Each one breaks up the white light.
They all make the same colors —
red, orange, yellow, green, blue, indigo,
and violet.
Here's a way to remember the colors.
The first letters of the colors spell the name
Roy G. Biv.

You can also make a rainbow.

DO IT YOURSELF

Make a Rainbow

Wait for a bright, sunny day.
Get a baking pan with sides about one or two
inches high.
Fill it nearly to the top with water.
Let the sun shine on it through a window.
Hold a small mirror in the pan.
Keep part in the water.
Keep part out of the water.
Lean the mirror so that the sun strikes it.
Look at the wall or ceiling above the window.
Do you see a rainbow of different colors?

If not:

- wait until the water becomes still.
- change the slant of the mirror.
- move the pan backward or forward.

Now, do you see the rainbow?

The mirror and water broke the light into different colors.
But you can put them back together.

DO IT YOURSELF

Mixing Colors

Cut out a four-inch circle of white cardboard.
Draw a straight line up and down.
Draw a line across the middle.
This should make four pie-shaped wedges.
Color one wedge red.
One wedge yellow.
One wedge blue.
Leave one wedge white.

Find a long pencil with a point.
Push the point up through the center of the circle.
Hold the pencil between the open palms of your hands.
Rub it back and forth very fast.
The colors will blend together.
And soon the disk will look white!

Colors can also trick your eyes.
Here are a few examples.

DO IT YOURSELF

Trick Your Eyes

Here are two squares of orange.
One has a white border.
One has a black border.
Which orange square is darker?

The square with the white border looks darker.
But it is not.
Both squares are the same.
Just the borders make them look different.

Here are three blue birds.
Stare at them and count to 50.
Then quickly look at a blank white wall
or ceiling.
Did you see three orange birds?

Staring at the blue birds made your eyes tired.
You could no longer see the color blue.
Then you looked at a white wall or ceiling.
Your eyes couldn't see the color blue in the white.
It saw a mix of other colors.
So the birds looked orange!

We need light to see.
But light has other uses.
Light from the sun helps green plants to grow.

Without sunlight we would have no food.
We eat fruits and vegetables that grow on plants.
And we eat the meat of animals that eat plants.

DEAD LEAVES

COAL

OIL

Light also gives us fuels.
Sunlight helped plants grow millions of years ago.
These plants died.
They were buried.
In time, they became coal, oil, and natural gas.

Today we burn these fuels to:

- keep us warm in the winter.
- drive our cars and trucks.
- help produce electricity.

The sun gives us light during the day.
But what happens after the sun sets?
How do we get light at night?

People have found many ways to make light.
At first they made light with fires and torches.
Later they made oil lamps, candles, and gaslights.
Now we also use electric lights.

Today we also have a very special kind of light.
This light is much brighter than any other light.
It is called a laser.

You can see lasers inside supermarket checkout
counters.
They read the pattern of lines on each label.

You can't see the lasers inside telephone wires.
But they carry voice signals for thousands of miles.

Doctors use laser beams to perform some operations.
Factories use lasers to drill holes and cut steel.

From:

- candles to lasers,
- lenses to colors,
- reflections to rainbows,

light is truly amazing!